DAILY PRAYER FROM THE WORLD'S FAITHS

REV ANDY ROLAND

WHY BOTHER WITH THIS BOOK?

You will discover new and interesting prayers.

You will appreciate the spirituality of your colleagues, friends and neighbours of other faiths.

You will gain insights into world news.

You will be blessed.

DAILY PRAYERS

FROM THE WORLD'S FAITHS

**REV ANDY ROLAND
AND FRIENDS**

Published by Filament Publishing Ltd
14 Croydon Road, Waddon, Croydon, Surrey, CR0 4PA

The right of Andrew Roland to be identified as the author of this work has been asserted by him in accordance with the Design and Copyright Act 1988.

© Andrew Roland 2023

Printed by T J Books

ISBN 978-1-915465-33-7

This book is protected by international copyright and may not be copied in any way without the prior written permission of the publishers.

CONTENTS

What they say	1
Because it's there	3
Introduction	5
How to use this book	9
Thanks	13

Daily Prayers from the World's Faiths

1 - Foundations	15
2 - Welcoming the Day	21
Teaspoon Prayers - Introduction	25
3 - Thanks	29
4 - Sorry	33
5 - Please	37
6 - At Night	41
7 - Surrender	45
Scriptures for the birth of Christ	49

Descriptions of the Faiths

An Introduction	53
Hinduism	57
Buddhism	63
Judaism	67
Western Christianity	71
Eastern Christianity	75
Islam	79
Sikhism	83
Alcoholics Anonymous	87

And more

Sikh Prayer	91
Photos	95
Other Books by Rev Andy	97

WHAT THEY SAY

"One of the deepest levels of interfaith encounter is reached when we understand how our neighbours and friends of different faiths express themselves in prayer before the One who is absolute in their own tradition. In this wide-ranging selection of prayers, Andy Roland, writing as a Christian, provides some varied trustworthy stepping stones for Christians who want to set off on that journey of appreciation in respect and humility."

**Rt Rev Dr Michael Ipgrave,
Bishop of Lichfield**

"One of the greatest privileges and most fascinating challenges for a Headteacher is how to lead the faith life of his or her school. As the Head of a cosmopolitan school in a cosmopolitan city, I feel particularly the need to build a faith life in which all my pupils can see themselves, and in which all are welcomed into the richness of a life led with spirituality. Rev Roland's new book will further inform that work, drawing on prayers from all the major religions, while also being reminded of the tenets that are held so warmly by all - gratitude, atonement, hope - or, as we are shown here 'thanks, sorry, please'. I look forward to sharing Rev Roland's work with my pupils and colleagues."

**Miss Amy Wallace, Principal,
Queens Gate School, SW7**

"This book would be good for R.E."
Edward age 12

BECAUSE IT'S THERE

In 1924 the mountaineer George Mallory set out to conquer Everest. Tragically, he died 240m from the summit.

Why did he do it?

It was Mallory's third Everest expedition. When he started out a reporter asked him just that question. Mallory simply replied, *"Because it's there."*

That is also the rationale for this small book. Why bother with the prayers of religions other than one's own?

The first reason is curiosity. We live in a multi-faith country in a multi-faith world. So how do other people pray? What does their religion look like from the inside?

The second reason is openness. Can I learn something from them? Can I even enrich my own prayers through the prayers of other faiths?

The third reason is relationships. It does no harm at all to have some knowledge about the faith of friends and acquaintances from other religious traditions.

Of course, we never stop learning. That's what makes life interesting. Enjoy the ride.

INTRODUCTION

MY FAMILY
I came into this world in the last days of the 1939-1945 war in Europe, with the surname Rosenbaum. My father was from a German Jewish family in Munich. He came over to study medicine in 1933 and changed his name to Roland when I was 2. My mother was from an impeccably English and Anglican background, but her religious commitment was as a Quaker. I was not baptised as a baby so I could make up my mind later, and, when at the age of 8 I was asked if I wanted to be baptised, I said yes. My father was an agnostic but respected all religions as did my mother. When they entertained someone of other faiths, the standard meal was fish, because no one had problems with that. My mother was much influenced by Mahatma Gandhi and by his spiritual successor Vinoba Bhave. An important book in the family house was a collection of prayers from different faiths called 'God of a Hundred Names', collected by Victor Gollancz. So I grew up in an atmosphere of positive attitudes to people from all sorts of faiths.

Mum and Dad went to Uganda for two years in 1957, my father working there as the first qualified ENT surgeon. They were involved in social programmes set up by the Aga Khan and supported both Quaker and Anglican pastors. My mother was a great supporter of the campaigns for independence of various African countries and against apartheid in South Africa. She founded the Rugby Africa Circle, the Coventry Africa Circle and the Leamington Africa Circle.

In the 1970's I went to a series of talks at the Catholic Church of Notre Dame in Leicester Square, London, where I heard a Hindu swami, a Muslim imam, a Jewish rabbi and an American Buddhist disciple talk separately about their faiths. Very enlightening. In 1983 I spent nine weeks in India, mostly in Tamil Nada and Kerala, exploring the interface between Christianity, Hinduism and Islam. When I was ordained and a curate in Streatham, I was a frequent visitor to the South London Synagogue. I am now retired, though busy writing, and now volunteer once a week as part of a multi-faith prison chaplaincy.

I realise that straight comparisons between religions are impossible. What I have found is that a religion is like a layer cake in which we find levels of resonance which can be a surprise, and levels of difference which can be equally surprising. The primary virtue to foster, I believe, is healthy curiosity.

LOCKDOWN

During the Covid pandemic in 2020 I decided to offer some spiritual resources to people on my email list. They included six collections of short prayers from each of the major faiths. I had completely forgotten about them until the end of 2022. When I looked them up again, I thought, *"There could be a book here."* So here it is.

FAITH FRIENDS

I know that if I were to offer something from another religion, I would inevitably see it through my own

Christian glasses. So I approached several people from the major faiths to seek their suggestions for the prayers. I am most grateful for the generosity and thoughtfulness they showed me.

I also realised that if the prayers were left to themselves, it would be easy to assume all faiths were thinking the same way. So working with my faith consultants I wrote a very brief summary of each of them, just 500 words. Writing the piece on Hinduism was a particular joy because I dug up my diaries from my time in India forty years ago and read some of the books I had brought back with me then. I rediscovered the spiritual warmth that is part and parcel of the Indian experience.

ALCOHOLICS ANONYMOUS
Eyebrows may be raised at my inclusion of Alcoholics Anonymous in the book, because it is emphatically not a religion. However, it is a spiritual path which Fr. Richard Rohr, from the Centre for Action and Contemplation, called *"a movement of the Spirit in our time."*

For the last five years of my time at Hackbridge and Beddington Corner, a vibrant 12-step group, Cocaine Anonymous, met every Tuesday in the church. I went along when I could because it was an open meeting, and I found it consistently inspiring. I particularly treasure the memory of one young man who described how he was tempted to use again and said, *"I just had to get down on my f...ing knees."*

It's a pretty good description of prayer.

HOW TO USE THIS BOOK

PIC N MIX
One way of using this book is simply browsing through it. You might say to yourself, 'I wonder what is the standard Muslim prayer; or how different is Eastern Christianity from Western; or what do Hindus say when they get up in the morning? I made so many discoveries through compiling this book, and I am sure you will too.

DAILY PRAYING
The book is designed so that you can follow one particular religion in starting and ending the day in prayer. Each religion is given a particular day of the week, so that you can follow the thread of that religion's prayer. But you don't have to do Buddhist prayer on Wednesday. The days of the week are simply a device, not an instruction.

SIMILARITIES AND DIFFERENCES
Prayers of all the major faiths have a commonality about them. They are after all at least in part human responses to universal situations. But they arise from particular world views and particular sets of beliefs, and so are dependent on history, geography, culture and climate as well as inspiring founders. So there are deep differences as well as deep similarities. The second section of the book is made up of very brief descriptions of each of the faiths, limited to about.

500 words each. (Hinduism, not surprisingly, took 780 words). I wrote them all, guided by a framework given me by my collaborator of each faith. I checked out the finished product with each of them. I hope that in each section you will find something to make you say, "I didn't know that."

I will end this section with the traditional Spanish farewell: *"Vade con Dios - Go with God."*

THANKS

My sincerest thanks to all who helped me to find an appropriate tone to the prayers and descriptions of the faiths represented here.

All mistakes and misapprehensions are entirely the responsibility of the author, Andy Roland.

In the order of the antiquity of each faith, these are:

- Dr Mattur Nandakumara MBE, Executive Director of the Bhavan Cultural Centre;
- Mr Gulu Anand, a director of the Hindu Council UK and trustee of Shree Ram Mandir, Southall;
- Lelung Rinpoche of the Lelung Dharma Centre;
- Rabbi Helen Freeman, Joint Senior Rabbi at the West London Synagogue;
- Fr Dobromir, Priest at the Bulgarian embassy;
- Fr Ian Graham, Priest at the Holy Trinity Greek Orthodox parish, Oxford;
- Professor Muhammad Abdel-Haleem OBE, Professor of Islamic Studies at SOAS, the School of Oriental and African Studies;
- Imam Siddiq, Chaplain;
- Gurchuran Singh, of the Gurdwara Sri Guru Singh Sabha Southall;
- Gagandeep Singh, Chaplain.

DAILY PRAYERS FROM THE WORLD'S FAITHS
1 - FOUNDATIONS OF FAITH

The opening theme is 'Foundations' - those prayers which members of faith communities take for granted within their own tradition but know little about from other traditions.

May you find what is here a blessing.

SUNDAY

✝ CHRISTIAN - WESTERN

Our Father, who art in heaven,
hallowed be thy name;
Thy kingdom come,
thy will be done in earth as it is in heaven.
Give us this day our daily bread;
Forgive us our trespasses,
as we forgive those who trespass against us
and lead us not into temptation,
but deliver us from evil.
(For thine is the kingdom, the power and the glory,
for ever and ever. Amen)

The Lord's Prayer, as it is called, was taught by Jesus to his disciples, as in Matthew 6.9-13. In the sixth and seventh lines, Matthew uses 'debts' not 'trespasses'.

The last two lines in brackets are not included in the oldest manuscripts, and may have come from 1 Chronicles 29.11.

There is a shorter and arguably more original version in Luke 11.2-4.

Monday

ॐ HINDU

> Aum - shantih, shantih, shantih
> Lead us from the unreal to the real.
> Lead us from darkness to light.
> Lead us from death to immortality.
> Aum - shantih, shantih, shantih.

(from Brihadaranyaka Upanishad 1.3.28)

Note:
The sound 'Aum' or 'Om' is an invocation to the Supreme Spirit. 'Shantih' means peace.

Tuesday

ALCOHOLICS ANONYMOUS

> Our description of the addict, the chapter to the agnostic, and our personal adventures before and after make clear three pertinent ideas:
>
> (a) that we were addicts and could not manage our own lives;

(b) that probably no human power could have relieved our addiction;

(c) that God could and would if he were sought.
(Alcoholics Anonymous, p.60)

I have replaced the word 'alcoholic' with the word 'addict', because over the last eighty years the twelve step programme of Alcoholics Anonymous has been adopted by countless groups of people suffering from a wide variety of addictions, from substance abuse like cocaine to mental processes like gambling.

WEDNESDAY

✵ BUDDHIST

The four Noble Truths were, according to tradition, spelled out in Gautama Buddha's first sermon after receiving enlightenment. There are countless ways of interpreting them.

The truth of suffering

The truth of desire - desire and ignorance are at the root of suffering

The truth of the end of suffering - either here or hereafter

The truth of the Noble Eightfold Path, namely
- Right understanding
- Right thought
- Right Speech
- Right Action
- Right Livelihood
- Right Effort
- Right Mindfulness
- Right Concentration

A good start is to sit upright for a certain length of time and concentrate on breathing deeply.

THURSDAY

✝ CHRISTIAN - EASTERN

> Lord Jesus Christ, Son of God, have mercy upon me, a sinner.

The Jesus prayer has been a cornerstone of Orthodox spirituality for at least six hundred years. It is used as a means of praying continually, so that it starts to run automatically at the back of one's mind, keeping one focused on God through Jesus. In recent years it has become popular among Western Christians as a form of meditation. It comes from the prayer of the blind beggar Bartimaeus in Mark 10.47, and the prayer of the tax collector in Jesus' parable in Luke 18.13.

FRIDAY

☾ MUSLIM

> In the name of Allah, the Beneficent, the Merciful.
> Praise be to Allah, Lord of the Worlds,
> The Beneficent, the Merciful.
> Master of the Day of Judgment,
> Thee alone we worship; Thee alone we ask for help.
> Show us the straight path,
> The path of those whom Thou hast favoured;
> Not the path of those who earn Thine anger nor of those who go astray.

Interpretation in English of Surah al-Fatihah (The Opening, the first Surah or chapter of the Qu'ran by Pickthall, 1930).

SATURDAY

♦ JEWISH

> Hear, O Israel: The Lord is our God, the Lord alone. You shall love the Lord your God with all your heart, and with all your soul, and with all your might. Keep these words that I am commanding you today in your heart. Recite them to your children and talk about them when you are at home and when you are away, when you lie down and when you rise. Bind them as a sign on your hand, fix them as an emblem on your forehead, and write them on the doorposts of your house and on your gates.

(Deuteronomy 6.4-9)

The Shema - so-called after the Hebrew for the first word - is the foundation of the Jewish faith. It is the centrepiece of morning and evening prayers. Observant Jews write it in a mezuzah and fix it to the entrance of their house.

It is quoted by Jesus when he was asked about the greatest commandment of the Law (Mark 12.28-34).

DAILY PRAYERS FROM THE WORLD'S FAITHS
2 - WELCOMING THE DAY

Sunday

✝ CHRISTIAN - WESTERN

Almighty and everlasting God,
I thank you that you have brought me safely
to the beginning of this day.
Keep me from falling into sin
or running into danger,
order me in all my doings
and guide me to do always
what is right in your sight.

(1552 Book of Common Prayer, altd. Used in 'Discovering Psalms as Prayer')

Monday

ॐ HINDU

All be happy
All be without disease
All creatures have well-being
And none be in misery of any sort

May peace and peace and peace be everywhere

(Traditionally to be said first thing every morning).

TUESDAY

ⓐ ALCOHOLICS ANONYMOUS

On awakening let us think about the twenty-four hours ahead. We consider our plans for the day. Before we begin, we ask God to direct our thinking, especially that it be divorced from self-pity, dishonest or self-seeking motives.

We ask especially for freedom from self-will and are careful to make no requests for ourselves only.

(Alcoholics Anonymous, p.86-87)

WEDNESDAY

❈ BUDDHIST

I am grateful that I have woken and am still breathing. May my day be meaningful.

(H.E. Lelung Rinpoche)

THURSDAY

† CHRISTIAN - EASTERN

Creator of the morning,
who drives out the darkness
and brings light and joy to all creation:
create in us habits of virtue,
and drive away from us all
the darkness of sin.
With the light give us joy

by the glorious rays of your grace,
Lord our God for ever. Amen

(Syrian Orthodox, from the liturgy of Kurisumula Ashram, a Benedictine monastery in Kerala, India. Quoted in 'Discovering Psalms as Prayer' by Andy Roland)

FRIDAY

☪ MUSLIM

We have entered a new day and with it all dominion is Allah's.
Praise is to Allah.
None has the right to be worshipped but Allah alone,
Who has no partner.
To Allah belongs the dominion,
and to Him is the praise and He is able to do all things.
My Lord, I ask You for the goodness of this day and of the days that come after it,
and I seek refuge in You from the evil of this day and of the days that come after it.
My Lord, I seek refuge in You from laziness and helpless old age.
My Lord, I seek refuge in You from the punishment of Hell-fire, and from the punishment of the grave.

(Day 3 of the morning prayers, from website Islamic Prayers)

SATURDAY

✡ JEWISH

Blessed are you, O Lord our God, King of the universe,
who creates your world every morning afresh.

(Contemporary, from 'God of a Hundred Names', p.19)

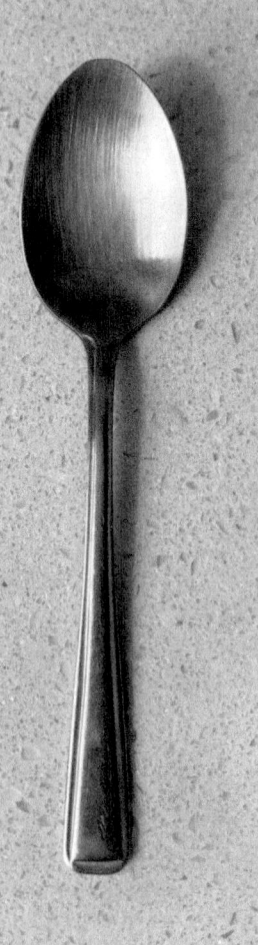

TEASPOON PRAYERS

When I was still vicar of Hackbridge and Beddington Corner, (between Croydon and Sutton in Greater London), I held a weekly lunchtime Bible meditation group in our Community Centre. At the end, we would pass a teaspoon round the circle, just like the Native American pipe of peace, and whoever had hold of it could say a prayer. We could of course have used a pen or a fork or a jam doughnut, but a teaspoon was particularly appropriate. Why? Because it enshrines the formula for normal prayer.

The reason for this is because the normal abbreviation for 'teaspoon' in recipe books is 'tsp'. This simply stands for Thanks, Sorry, Please. In that order.

Saying thank you to God instantly puts us into the right relationship with him. And it is psychologically healthy for us to live with 'an attitude of gratitude'.

The next step is to face up to reality where we have wilfully or inadvertently failed or been self-centred. Luther coined the memorable phrase, *"Sin boldly"*. In other words recognise where you have stumbled, but don't stay there. Someone once asked a monk in the Egyptian desert what they did in their monastery. He replied, *"We fall and get up, fall and get up, fall and get up."*

Finally we change our focus from God and us to God and others. You may be aware of crunching of internal gears at this point. I have a very simple prayer which is appropriate for friends and enemies: *"Lord, bless x and give them what they need."*

With these three you have covered most of the bases. They are the headings for the next three sections.

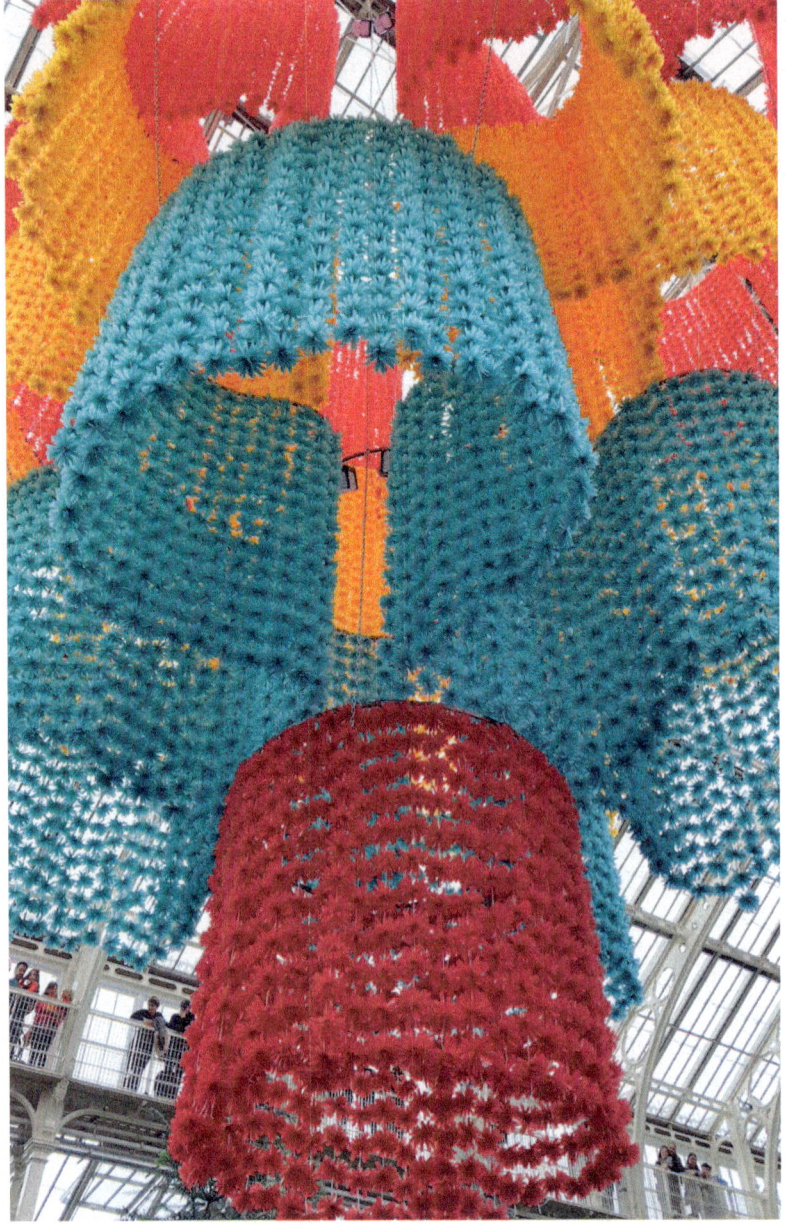

DAILY PRAYERS FROM THE WORLD'S FAITHS
3 - THANKS

SUNDAY

✝ CHRISTIAN - WESTERN

Thanks be to you, O Lord Jesus Christ.
for all the benefits you have given to me,
for all the pains and insults you have borne for me.
O most merciful redeemer, friend and brother,
may I know you more clearly,
love you more dearly,
and follow you more nearly,
day by day.

(First half from St Richard of Chichester, d.1253)

MONDAY

ॐ HINDU

When a person surrenders all desires that come to the heart and by the grace of God finds the joy of God, then their soul has indeed found peace.

(Bhagavad Gita - Song of God - 2.55)

TUESDAY
ⓐ ALCOHOLICS ANONYMOUS

An honest regret for harms done, a genuine gratitude for blessings received, and a willingness to try for better things tomorrow will be the permanent assets we shall seek.

(12 Steps and 12 Traditions, p.95)

Keep an Attitude of Gratitude.

(Traditional)

WEDNESDAY
☸ BUDDHIST

Health is the greatest possession. Contentment is the greatest treasure. Confidence is the greatest friend. Nirvana (liberation) is the greatest joy.

When a person knows the solitude of silence, and feels the joy of quietness, they are the free from fear and sin and they feel the joy of the Dhamma (cosmic order/the Buddha's teachings).

(Dhammapada v. 204, 205)

THURSDAY
✝ CHRISTIAN - EASTERN

We, your thankful and unworthy servants, praise and glorify you, O Lord, for your great benefits which we have received; we bless you, we thank you, we sing to you and we magnify your great goodness, and in humility and love we worship you: O Benefactor and Saviour, glory to you.

(Manual of Eastern Orthodox Prayers [1945], p.20)

Friday

☪ ISLAM

> Praise be to Him who when I call on Him answers me,
> slow though I am when He calls me.
> Praise be to Him who gives to me when I ask Him,
> miserly though I am when he asks a loan of me.
> Praise be to Him to whom I confide my needs
> whenever I will,
> and he satisfies me.
> My Lord I praise, for He is of my praise most worthy.

(Prayer and Meditation [1971] - F C Happold, p.63)

Saturday

✡ JUDAISM

> We declare with gratitude that You are our God and
> the God of our fathers forever.
> You are our rock, the rock of our life and the shield
> that saves us…
>
> At every moment, at evening, morning and noon,
> we experience your wonders and your goodness.
> You are goodness itself, for Your mercy has no
> end. You are mercy itself, for your love has no limit.
> Forever have we put our hope in you.

(Forms of Prayer for Jewish Worship, Reform Synagogues of G.B., p,237)

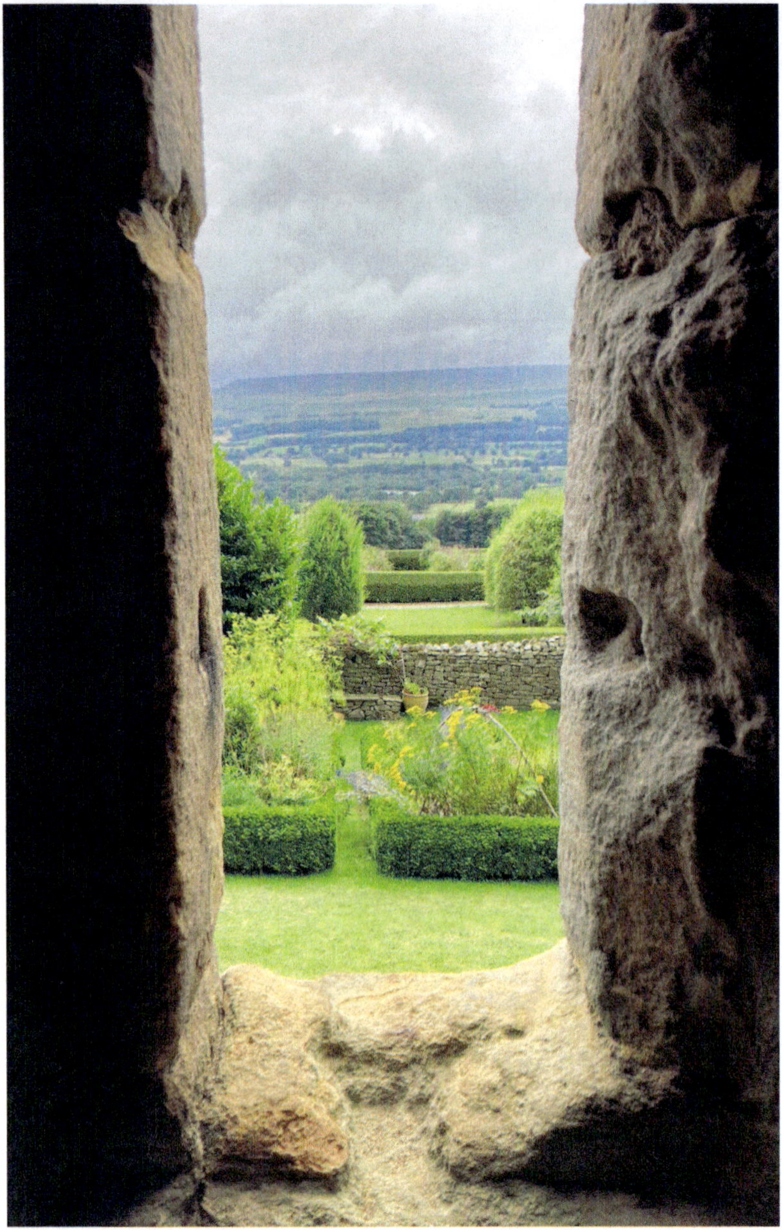

DAILY PRAYERS FROM THE WORLD'S FAITHS
4 - SORRY

SUNDAY

✝ CHRISTIAN - WESTERN

O thou great Chief, light a candle in my heart
and sweep the rubbish from thy dwelling place.

(a Nigerian schoolgirl, from the Oxford Book of Prayers)

MONDAY

ॐ HINDU

Hate and lust for things of nature have their roots
in man's lower nature. Let him not fall under their
power: they are the two enemies in his path.
Know him who is above reason; and let his peace
give thee peace. Be a warrior and kill desire, the
powerful enemy of the soul.

(Bhagavad Gita - Song of God - 3.34, 43, trans Juan Mascaro)

TUESDAY

ⓐ ALCOHOLICS ANONYMOUS

Selfishness - self-centredness! That, we think, is the root of our troubles. Driven by a hundred forms of fear, self-delusion, self-seeking and self-pity, we step on the toes of our fellows and they retaliate… Above everything, we alcoholics must be rid of this selfishness. God makes that possible. And there often seems no way of getting rid of self without his aid.

(Alcoholics Anonymous, p. 62)

WEDNESDAY

☸ BUDDHIST

Do not do what is evil. Do what is good. Keep your mind pure. This is the teaching of the Buddha.

(Dhammapada v 185)

THURSDAY

☦ CHRISTIAN - EASTERN

Have mercy on me, O God,
according to your steadfast love;
according to your abundant mercy
blot out my transgressions…

Create in me a clean heart, O God,
and put a new and right spirit within me…

Restore to me the joy of your salvation,
and sustain in me a willing spirit.

(Psalm 50. 1, 10, 12. In Protestant Bibles it is Psalm 51)

In several Orthodox churches, including the Syrian

Orthodox Church, Psalm 50.1-17 is said every morning. I discovered the power of this and other psalms when I visited a Benedictine Ashram in Kerala, South India many years ago. I still use them, as I describe in 'Discovering Psalms as Prayer'.

Friday

☪ ISLAM

Our Lord! Condemn us not if we forget or fall into error.
Our Lord! Lay not on us a burden like that which You did lay on those before us.
Our Lord! Lay not on us a burden greater than we have strength to bear.
Blot out our sins, and grant us forgiveness.
Have mercy on us. You are our Protector.
Help us against those who stand against faith.

(Qu'ran 2.286)

Saturday

✡ JUDAISM

"How does one confess? They say: 'Please God! I have intentionally sinned, I have sinned out of lust and emotion, and I have sinned unintentionally. I have done [such-and-such] and I regret it, and I am ashamed of my deeds, and I shall never return to such a deed.' That is the essence of confession, and all who are frequent in confessing and take great value in this matter, indeed are praiseworthy."

(Maimonides [1135 - 1204] from his 'Mishneh Torah')

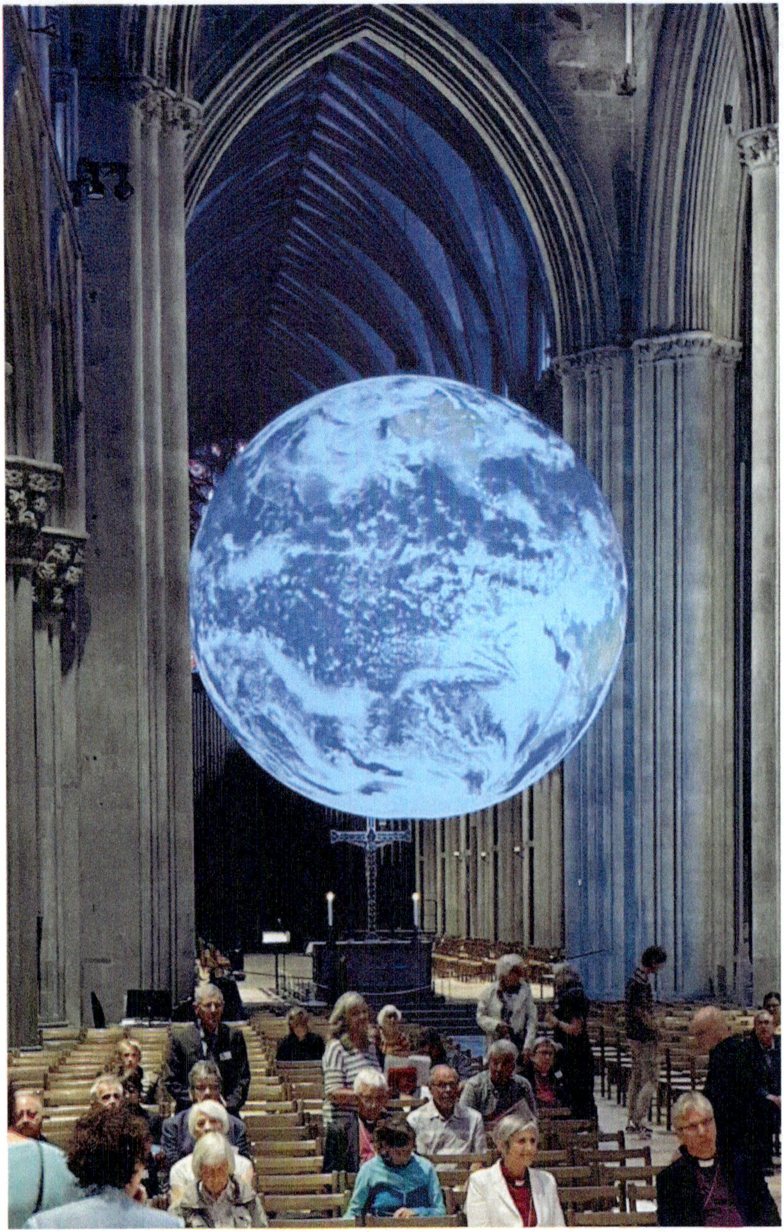

DAILY PRAYERS FROM THE WORLD'S FAITHS
5 - PLEASE

Sunday

✝ CHRISTIAN - WESTERN

Watch, dear Lord, with those who wake, or watch, or weep tonight, and give your angels charge over those who sleep. Look after your sick ones, O Lord Christ; give rest to your weary ones; bless your dying ones; soothe your suffering ones; shield your joyous ones; and all for your Love's sake.

(St Augustine of Hippo, 354 - 430)

Monday

ॐ HINDU

Show love to all creatures, and you will be happy. For when you love all things, you love the Lord, for he is all in all.

(Tulsi Das, 1532 - 1623)

Tuesday

ⓐ ALCOHOLICS ANONYMOUS

We ask especially for freedom from self-will, and are careful to make no requests for ourselves only. We may ask for ourselves, however, if others are to be helped.

(Alcoholics Anonymous, p. 87)

Wednesday

☸ BUDDHIST

From my own limited experience I have found that the greatest degree of inner tranquility comes from the development of love and compassion. The more we care for the happiness of others, the greater our own sense of well-being becomes. Cultivating a close, warm-hearted feeling for others automatically puts the mind at ease. This helps remove whatever fears or insecurities we may have and gives us the strength to cope with any obstacles we encounter. It is the ultimate source of success in life.

(14th Dalai Lama)

Thursday

✝ CHRISTIAN - EASTERN

We offer you, we your servants, prayers and intercessions for the peace of the world and the reconciliation of all nations. We pray on behalf of all living creatures who are afflicted or oppressed, and who look to you for relief. Make us all work with you for the removal of evil, that the human

family may rise from its enslavement to sin, that true
freedom reign among the people, and justice with
love prevail all over the world…"

(Syrian Orthodox Liturgy, 'The Harp of the Spirit' p.86)

FRIDAY

☪ ISLAM

The quickest answered prayer (du'a) is the prayer in secret for another person.

(Ibn Taymiyyah)

SATURDAY

✡ JUDAISM

May great peace from heaven, life and fulfilment,
salvation and consolation, healing and redemption,
forgiveness and atonement, relief and deliverance
be granted to us and to all the family of Israel.
Amen.

(from the Hebrew Kaddish)

Happy are those whose help is the God of Jacob,
whose hope is in the Lord their God…
Who executes justice for the oppressed, who gives
food to the hungry.
The Lord sets the prisoners free, the Lord opens the
eyes of the blind.
The Lord lifts up those who are bowed down; the
Lord loves the righteous.
The Lord watches over the strangers, he upholds
the orphan and the widow,
But the way of the wicked he brings to ruin.

(Psalm 146.5, 7-9)

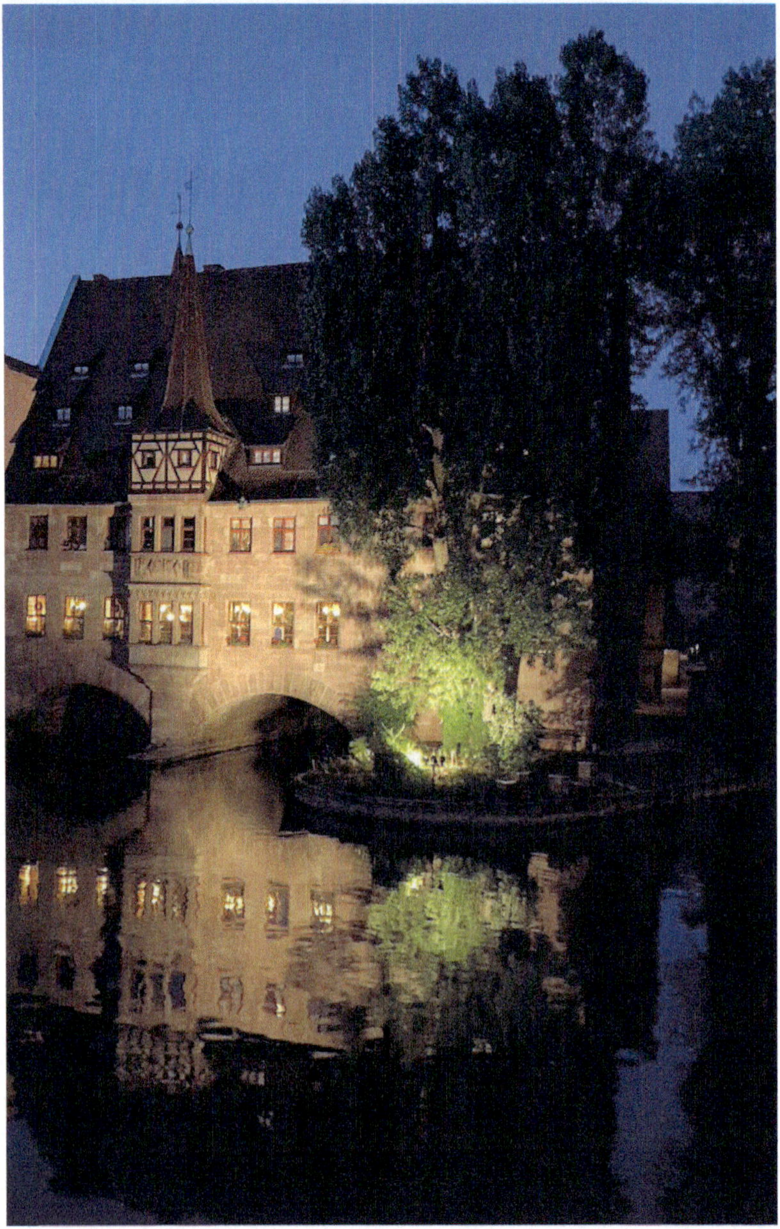

DAILY PRAYERS FROM THE WORLD'S FAITHS
6 - AT NIGHT

SUNDAY

✝ CHRISTIAN - WESTERN

Lighten our darkness, Lord, we pray,
and in your great mercy
defend us from all perils and dangers of this night,
for the love of your only Son,
our Saviour Jesus Christ.

(Night Prayer/Compline, in most churches)

MONDAY

ॐ HINDU

O Lord, kindly forgive my wrong actions done knowingly or unknowingly;
either through my organs of action (hands, feet, speech),
or through my organs of perception (ears, eyes),
or by my mind.
Glory unto Thee, O Lord, who is the ocean of kindness.

(from Hindu blog by Abhilash Rajendran)

TUESDAY

ⓐ ALCOHOLICS ANONYMOUS

When we retire at night, we constructively review our day. Were we resentful, selfish, dishonest or afraid? Do we owe an apology?… Were we kind and loving towards all? What could we have done better?… After making our review we ask God's forgiveness and inquire what corrective measures should be taken.

(Alcoholics Anonymous p.85)

WEDNESDAY

✸ BUDDHIST

Meditation:
My mind is calm and my body is relaxed.
I am at peace.
I am calm and my body is still.
I welcome sleep into my being.
I breathe in peace and I breathe out stress.
My mind and body are ready to sleep.

(from univers-bouddha.com)

THURSDAY

✝ CHRISTIAN (EASTERN)

Into thy hands, O Lord Jesus Christ, my God, I commend my spirit; do thou bless me, have mercy upon me, and grant me eternal life. Amen

(A Manual of Eastern Orthodox Prayers p.19)

Friday

☪ ISLAM

> O Allah, verily You have created my soul
> and You shall take its life, to You belongs its life and death.
> If You should keep my soul alive then protect it,
> and if You should take its life then forgive it.
> O Allah, I ask You to grant me good health.'

(Supplication before sleeping)

Saturday

🕎 JUDAISM

> O Eternal, may it be Your will that I lie down in peace and rise up in peace. Let not my thoughts, my dreams, or my daydreams disturb me. Watch over my family and those I love. O Guardian of Israel, who neither slumbers nor sleeps, I entrust my spirit to You.

(University of Pennsylvania, Selected Jewish Prayers and Blessings)

GOOD NIGHT

The following charming night time Swahili blessing comes from Tanzania:

> "La la salaama" - "Sleep well."

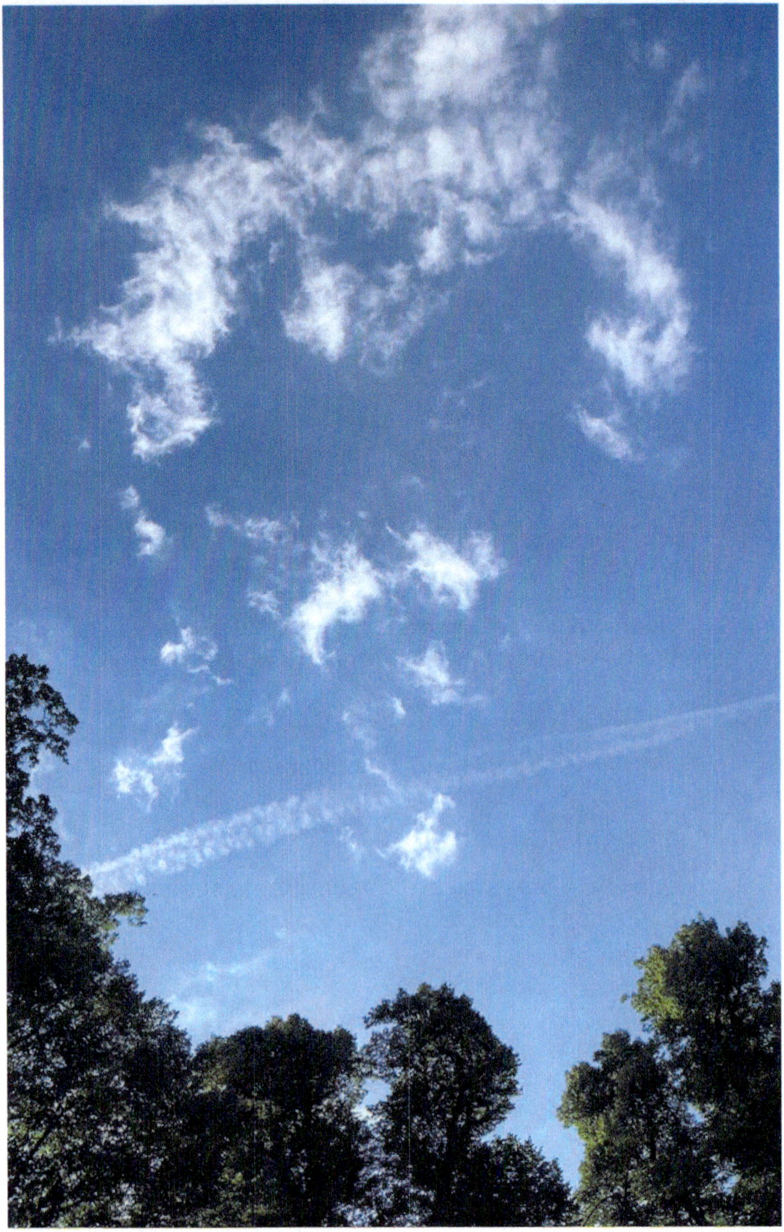

DAILY PRAYERS FROM THE WORLD'S FAITHS
7 - SURRENDER

The fundamental religious attitude is of dependence on a higher, spiritual power. This is expressed in all the world's faiths, and typically results in an openness to help others.

Sunday
✝ CHRISTIAN - WESTERN
Take, O Lord, and receive all my liberty, my memory, my understanding, and my entire will. Whatever I have or hold, You have given me; I restore it all to You and surrender it wholly to be governed by Your will. Give me only Your love and Your grace, and I am rich enough and ask for nothing more.

(St Ignatius of Loyola, 1481-1556)

Monday
ॐ HINDU
When a person surrenders all desires that come to the heart, and by the grace of God finds the joy of

God, then his soul has indeed found peace.

(Bhagavad Gita 2.55)

TUESDAY

ⓐ ALCOHOLICS ANONYMOUS

God, I offer myself to Thee, to build with me and to do with me as Thou wilt. Relieve me from the bondage of self, that I may better do Thy will. Take away my difficulties, that victory over them may bear witness to those I would help of Thy Power, Thy Love, Thy Way of life. May I do Thy will always.

(Alcoholics Anonymous, p. 63)

WEDNESDAY

☸ BUDDHIST

Leaving behind the path of darkness and following the path of light, let the wise man leave his home life and go into a life of freedom. In solitude that few enjoy, let him find his joy supreme: free from possessions, free from desires, and free from whatever may darken the mind.

(Dhammapada v86, 87)

THURSDAY

† CHRISTIAN - EASTERN

O Lord, by the power of the grace of the Holy Spirit, vouchsafe that we may live according to Thy holy will.

(Staretz Silouan of Mt. Athos, 1866 - 1932)

Friday

☪ ISLAM

Oh Allah! I surrender myself to you. You are the One who created me, the One who knows my pains and my hidden tears, the One who sees everything hidden and untold. Oh Allah! Forgive me, guide me, have mercy on me.

(from Pinterest, Beautiful Islamic Quotes)

Saturday

🕎 JUDAISM

Turn us back to Your teaching, our father, and draw us near to Your service, our king. Bring us back in perfect repentance to Your presence. Blessed are You Lord, who desires repentance.

(from the Daily Amidah, Forms of Prayer for Jewish Worship, p. 235)

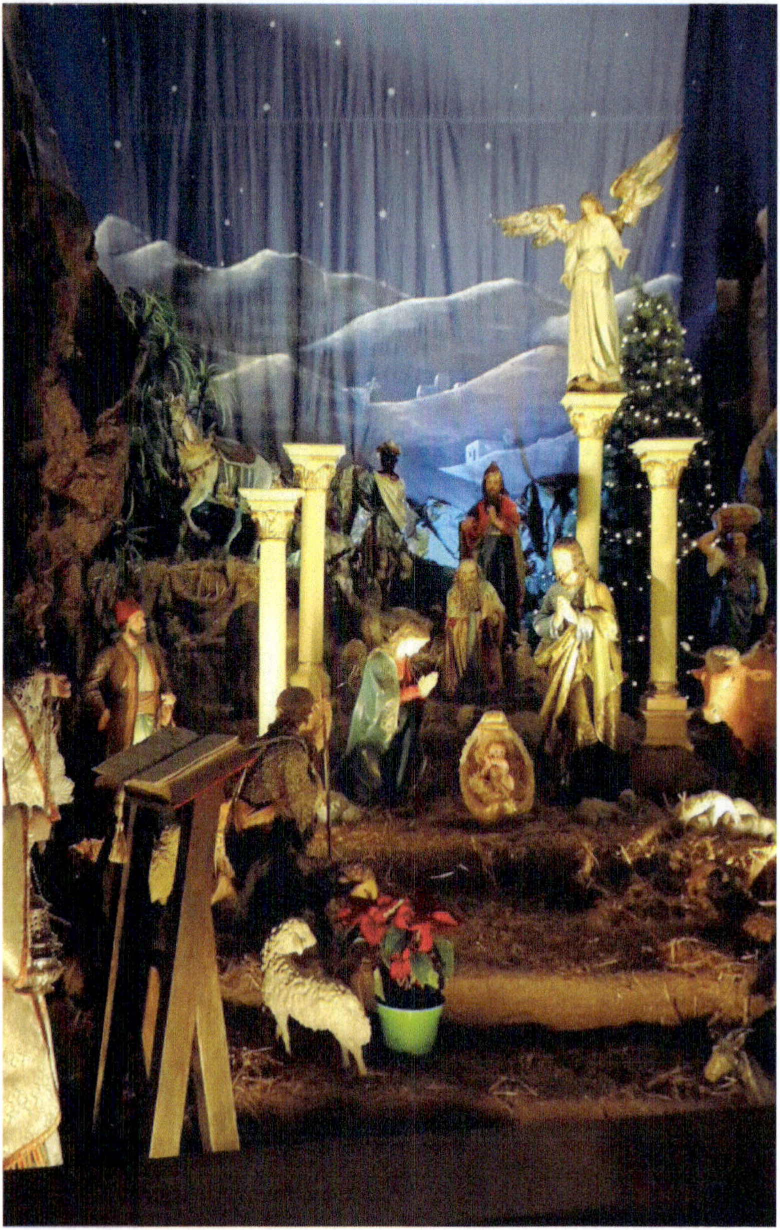

SCRIPTURES FROM AROUND THE WORLD FOR THE BIRTH OF CHRIST

Several times while I was vicar of Hackbridge and Beddington Corner, I included passages from Muslim and Hindu scriptures in the Christmas Service of Nine Lessons and Carols. I felt it was a time when the resonances outweighed the dissonances. See what you think.

DECEMBER 20TH

✝ A CHRISTIAN PRAYER

Almighty and everlasting God,
Who stooped to raise fallen humanity
Through the child-bearing of blessed Mary;
Grant that we, who have seen your glory
revealed in our human nature,
may follow the way of your Son Jesus Christ.

(Collect of the Blessed Virgin Mary, altd.)

DECEMBER 21ST

ॐ A HINDU SCRIPTURE

Although I am unborn, the Lord of all living entities,
and have an imperishable nature, yet I appear in

this world by virtue of my divine power.
Whenever there is a decline in righteousness and
an increase in unrighteousness,
at that time I manifest myself on earth.
To protect the righteous, to annihilate the wicked,
and to reestablish the principles of virtue (dharma),
I appear on this earth, age after age.

(Bhagavad Gita 4.6-8)

DECEMBER 22ND

☸ BUDDHIST WISDOM

All the joy the world contains has come through
wishing happiness for others.
All the misery the world contains has come through
wanting pleasure for oneself.

(Śāntideva, The Way of the Bodhisattva)

DECEMBER 23RD

♈ A JEWISH HOPE

For a child has been born for us, a son given to us;
authority rests upon his shoulders; and he is named
Wonderful Counsellor, Mighty God, Everlasting
Father, Prince of Peace.

(Isaiah 9.6)

DECEMBER 24TH

☪ A MUSLIM WITNESS

And mention in the Book Maryam, when she
withdrew from her family to a place toward the
east. Then We sent to her Our Angel, and he

represented himself to her as a well-proportioned man. She said, "Indeed, I seek refuge in the Most Merciful from you, if you should be fearing of Allah." He said, "I am only the messenger of your Lord to give you a pure boy." She said,"How can I have a boy while no man has touched me and I have not been unchaste?" He said, "Thus your Lord says, 'It is easy for Me, and We will make him a sign to the people and a mercy from Us. And it is a matter decreed.' "

(The Qu'ran, Surah Maryam, 19:16-21)

December 25th

✝ THE MEANING OF CHRISTMAS

In the beginning was the Word, and the Word was with God, and the Word was God…

In him was life, and the life was the light of all people…

And the Word became flesh and lived among us, and we have seen his glory, the glory as of a father's only son, full of grace and truth.

(John 1.1, 4, 14)

BRIEF DESCRIPTIONS OF THE FAITHS - AN INTRODUCTION

There are two equal and opposite mistakes that we can fall into when considering other faiths. One is to think that all religions say the same thing only in different words. The other is to say that they have nothing in common; that to be curious about another's religion is to betray one's own faith.

What I have discovered in my encounter with other faiths was the constant element of surprise. Surprise at resonances when we seem to speak the same language. And then surprise at the dissonances between us.

I had an example of resonance when I had a debate at Kingston University with Sheikh Zaki Badawi, Chief Imam of the Central London Mosque, over Salman Rushdie's 'Satanic Verses'. I remember the confusion on the faces of the Muslim students because Zaki Badawi and I kept agreeing with each other.

An example of dissonance is a discussion I had with four charming Hindu men in the Meenakshi Sundaraswarar temple in Madurai. I was trying to get across to them the idea of sin, and I asked, *"What makes Siva angry?"* It was just as if I had asked, *"How square is yellow?"* So I asked what would happen if a man got rid of his wife by killing her in one of those fake bride-burning kitchen 'accidents'. *"Oh,"* they replied, *"he'll be punished in this life!"* *"Hello'"* I thought, *"what's happened to karma?"* Of course what they were saying was explicitly a statement about karma.

One of my most enlightening experiences was attending a week of talks on other religions in the modern church of Notre Dame de France by Leicester Square London. I heard an account of Judaism by a rabbi, of Islam by an imam, of Hinduism by a swami, and of Buddhism by a young American monk. What became clear was how each religion provides its own way of looking at life and the emotional overtones that come with it. It is so easy for an outsider to get it wrong.

One Greenbelt Festival I heard a vicar speak of his friendship with a local imam. One day he was invited to speak at the mosque and someone asked him to talk about Christianity. As he did so, he realised that his friend the imam was sitting with his head in his hands. When the vicar asked him if he had said anything upsetting, the imam replied, *"Oh no. I just realised that I have been teaching my people the wrong things all these years."* And they were friends!

The following very brief descriptions were created in this way. I sat down with a member of the religion in question, normally the one whom I had consulted about their prayers. They gave me a framework for the description. I did my best to complete that in 500 words, which I then forwarded to them for their own comments and corrections. I hope that the following descriptions capture the flavour of each religion and can form a basis for mutual respect.

The religions are described in the order of their appearance on the world stage. So Hinduism comes first. It is the only religion I was unable to limit to 500 words. It is in fact 780 words. My apologies. The book ends with a substantial section of the most important Sikh prayer. Sikh prayers/hymns ('banis') are repeated each day for twenty five minutes. They cannot easily be broken down into shorter specific prayers, which is why they occur at the end and not in the earlier section of the book. It also an appropriately prayerful way to end.

ॐ

HINDUISM

THE FOUR ASPECTS OF RELIGION
(From 'Facets of Brahman or the Hindu Gods' by Swami Chidbhavananda.

1 - Philosophy
For over three thousand years Indian sages have explored how what underlies the cosmos can relate to the cosmos.

The Rig Vedas are the world's earliest religious writings, c.1500 BCE. It has over 100,000 Sanskrit verses and a thousand hymns, principally to the gods Indra, Agni and the ritual drink Soma. They describe rituals, and how to praise the gods; later Vedas consider philosophical questions. To Hindus the Vedas are 'sruti' or 'heard', i.e. direct revelations from Brahman, the source of everything.

The Upanishads are philosophical reflections on the relation between cosmic realities and humankind. There are 108 Upanishads, written between 800 and 300 BCE. Central concepts are Brahman, the Absolute, and Atman (breath), the spiritual principle which is within each person and within the entire cosmos. "Tat tvam asi' - 'Thou art that'. The Upanishads, including the Bhagavad Gita (Song of God) are 'smriti' which means 'remembered', i.e. secondary to the original revelation.

The two central concepts for Hindu life are 'karma' and 'moksha'. Karma is the eternal law of cause and effect, within and beyond this world. Moksha is the final liberation from the cycles of birth and death.

2 - Epics

India has two giant epics. The Mahbaharata is the longest poem in the world, centred on the civil war between royal cousins, the Pandavas and Kauravas. It includes the Bhagavad Gita, in which the Supreme God Vishnu takes the form (avatar) of the god/hero Krishna; he instructs the warrior Arjuna on the nature of the real and the unreal.

The Ramayana is much shorter. It tells of Rama's fourteen year exile in the forest, his return as king and the kidnapping of his wife Sita by the king of Sri Lanka. She is rescued with the help of the popular monkey god Hanuman, an avatar of Shiva.

3 - Puranas (myths and legends of the gods)

There are eighteen major Puranas, written around the first millennium CE. Some are advaita - non-dualist, i.e. all will be absorbed in the Absolute. Others are dvaita - dualist, i.e. what is created has reality and is able to relate to the Absolute through loving devotion. Shiva and Vishnu are both the Supreme God. Shiva's wife is Menakshi or Shakti (supreme spiritual power). Their eldest son, Ganesh or Ganapathy, is the onetusked elephant-headed god, to whom devotees pray for success in life. The black goddess Kali with a belt and necklace of bleeding human heads is the fierce form of Shakti and may represent the destructive power of time.

The three supreme Gods, the 'Trimurti', are Brahma the creator, Vishnu the preserver and Shiva, creator and destroyer. The last letters of their names define the sacred sound 'Om' as 'AUM': BrahmA, VishnU, Shiva Mahesh.

4 - Rituals
People worship at temples and wayside shrines by waving 'arati' (sacred fire) or offering food and garlands. Devotional songs or 'bhajans' are very popular. Homes have rituals too. A children's comic (1983) says, *"Look upon your mother and father as God… Touch the feet of your parents before you go to school everyday and seek their blessings."*

POPULAR SUPERSTITION
Many ways are practised to improve the present and future: astrology; fortune-telling, animal sacrifice, seeking out those with spiritual powers. Swami Nityananda of Thapovanam said these were the dark side of Hinduism, meaning the darkness of ignorance, of those of gross natures.

THE THREE PATHS
In the Bhagavad Gita Krishna describes the three paths or yogas by which one can attain 'moksha' or liberation from the cycles of birth and death.

Jnana Yoga
The path of wisdom, is to meditate until one sees the unreality of the phenomenal world (chapter 6).

Karma Yoga
The path of action, is to do one's work in a spirit of non-attachment, where everything is offered to God (chapter 3-5).

Bhakti Yoga
The way of loving devotion to any personal deity, *"Those who with pure love meditate on me and adore me - these I very soon deliver from the ocean of death and life-in-death"* (chapter 12).

LIFE IN SOCIETY
The Four Stages of Life
These are: the student, the householder, the retired forest-dweller, and finally the 'sanyassin', who renounces the world and focuses on the spiritual life.

The structure of society
The Rig Vedas describe four castes:

- Brahmins - priests;
- Kshatriyas - rulers, administrators, warriors;
- Vaishiyas - farmers, artisans, traders;
- Shudras - labourers.

Today in India there are 3,000 castes and 25,000 sub-castes. Modern urban society blurs the distinction between castes. Below the caste system are tribal people and 200 million Dalits or untouchables.

END THOUGHT
When asked how the mountain Arunachala could be God, an English devotee replied, *"Why not?"*

BUDDHISM

THE BUDDHA
About 500 BCE a prince was born in the border region of modern-day Nepal and India called Siddhartha Gautama. As a young man he abandoned his life of luxury and became a wandering monk, undertaking severe ascetic practices such as extreme fasting. After he realised that such practices were harmful rather than helpful, he advocated a 'middle way'. While meditating under a 'bodhi' tree near Varanasi, he attained enlightenment and eventually came to be known as the Buddha, the Awakened One. At first he had only five disciples, but his ideas gradually spread through India and beyond, particularly through the advocacy of Buddhist Indian emperors such as Ashoka (304-232 BCE).

THE FOUR NOBLE TRUTHS
Gautama Buddha's fundamental insight was the four noble truths:

- the truth of suffering, which is inevitable in this world of samsara or the endless cycles of deaths and rebirths;

- the truth of the causes of suffering, which arises through craving or desire;
- the truth of the cessation of suffering, through the renunciation or ending of desire;
- the truth of the Way or dharma, the eightfold path.

The eightfold path consists of right understanding, right thought, right speech, right action, right livelihood, right effort, right mindfulness, right consciousness (samadhi).

Fundamental to the Way or dharma is the practice of meditation, of focussing the mind to a single point, freeing one's consciousness from the world of *samsara*.

By following the eightfold path and realising the four noble truths, one becomes enlightened and liberated from the endless cycles of death and rebirth.

THE MAIN BUDDHIST SCHOOLS

The classification of the schools of Buddhism is vague due to the sheer number (perhaps thousands) of different sects, sub-sects, movements, etc. that have made up the whole of Buddhist traditions. The three main schools however are clear, Theravada, Mahayana and Tantriana (or Vajrayana).

Theravada

Theravada, meaning 'Teaching of the Elders', is mainly in Sri Lanka and south-east Asia. Its teachings are based on the oldest Buddhist writings, the Pali canon. The practice of Vipassana meditation has become very influential in the west under the name of mindfulness. In 2010 36% of Buddhists adhered to the Theravada way.

Mahayana

Mahayana, or Great Vehicle grew up in India in the 1st century BCE. It centres on bodhisattvas, those who seek buddhahood or enlightenment for the benefit of all sentient beings. In addition to earlier texts, it follows a collection of scriptures called the Mahayana sutras. It expanded around 500 CE, but disappeared from India because of the Muslim invasions which started in 712 BCE. It had already spread throughout eastern Asia, particularly China, Tibet and Japan where it remains the dominant religion. It includes the rigorous Zen meditation-practice and Pure Land Buddhism, which focusses on being reborn within Buddha's direct field of influence in just one lifetime. In 2010 Mahayana constituted 53% of Buddhists.

Tantriana/Vajrayana

Tantriana is a subset of Mahayana. It generally deals with new forms of meditation and ritual using visualisation of Buddhist deities (including Buddhas, bodhisattvas and fierce deities) and the use of mantra recitation and mandalas.

JUDAISM

PATRIARCHS AND MATRIARCHS

'The LORD said to Abram, "Go from your country and your kindred and your father's house to the land that I will show you" (Genesis 12.1). The obedience of Abram/Abraham and Sarai/Sarah to the mysterious call of God was the founding moment of Judaism. Hope for their own land was passed down to Abraham's son, grandson and great-grandson Joseph with his brothers. These were traditionally the founders of the twelve tribes of Israel. After living as immigrants/slaves in Egypt for four hundred years, Moses led them out to receive the Torah at Sinai and to conquer the land of Canaan.

TORAH

'Torah' means teaching, law, instruction. It often refers to the first books, Genesis, Exodus, Leviticus, Numbers and Deuteronomy. Every synagogue has a 'Sefer Torah', a hand-written copy of the these five books. As well as the written Torah, equally authoritative is the Oral Torah. This records the debates and decisions of the rabbis. The laws which define the community are called 'Halakha' and are seen as unalterable by Orthodox Judaism, but as general guidelines by Reform Judaism.

STUDY AND ACTION
Jews serve God by study, prayer and by the observance of the commandments in the Torah. These include abstaining from most activities on the Sabbath (Friday evening to Saturday evening), and observing the purity rules of kashrut/kosher. Studying how to apply Halakha to modern conditions is central, as is the practice of 'Chesed' or deeds of loving kindness.

COMMUNITY LIFE
Jewish life revolves around the home and the community. The home is 'a small sanctuary' where the Sabbath (Shabbat) and Passover (Pesach) are celebrated through food and ritual. Synagogues are the central institution for community prayer, study and religious festivals.

JEWISH HISTORY
Second Temple period
In 586 BCE Babylon destroyed Jerusalem and the Temple and took the people into exile. It was there that the Tanakh ('Old Testament') took shape. Later some returned and rebuilt the Temple. Judaea was part of the Persian empire until the Maccabean revolt in 166 BCE. Rome took control a hundred years later and appointed King Herod, who massively expanded the Temple, which was in turn destroyed in the revolt of 66-70 CE.

Talmud
After the destruction of Jerusalem, the oral teaching of the rabbis began to be collected, culminating in the Jerusalem Talmud c. 400 and the larger Babylonian Talmud c. 500 CE. It is the central text of rabbinic Judaism, with teachings and opinions of thousands of rabbis and is the basis of all codes of Jewish law.

Persecution and Dispersion
Large numbers of Jews settled throughout the Roman Empire. Christian hostility and sporadic persecution became the Jewish experience, with migrations to the Islamic world, to Western Europe, to Eastern Europe and Russia. This culminated in the Nazi Holocaust of 6 million dead.

Israel
In 1948 Jews in Palestine won an independent state of Israel for the first time in 1900 years. Hebrew became the national language. Tensions remain, between secular/liberal Israelis and the Orthodox/Haredim, as well as between Israel and those Palestinians Arabs remaining after the war of 1948 when some 700,00 were made refugees. As the Prime Minister Yitzhak Rabin said in September 1993, *"We are destined to live together, on the same soil in the same land."*

✝
WESTERN CHRISTIANITY

BEGINNINGS
'On the night he was betrayed, Jesus took bread and said, *"This is my body."* He then took a cup of wine and said, *"This is my blood of the covenant."* Less than twenty hours later he had died on a cross and after three days had been seen alive by his closest companions. Thus was born the Christian Church.

FIRST FOLLOWERS
Jesus (or rather Yeshua) was Jewish as were all his disciples. Only after a few years were non-Jews welcomed into the community. How the two groups should relate was the subject of most of the New Testament. Within a century the Church was very largely Gentile. This brought on 250 years of persecution, during which simply to be a Christian was punishable by death.

THE CHURCH VICTORIOUS
In 315 the Roman emperor Constantine became a Christian. The Church became established, popular and powerful. A series of church councils decided on

what was the right way to talk about God and Christ. Monastic communities grew up as centres of radical obedience to the words of Jesus. German tribes eventually overthrew the Western Roman Empire but in turn were incorporated into the Church.

THE EARLY MIDDLE AGES
Over the next five hundred years, English, German and Scandinavian peoples accepted the new faith. Churches, cathedrals and monasteries sprung up everywhere in Europe, as well as hospitals and universities. Pilgrimages and personal devotions increased, along with the power and prosperity of the Church.

THE REFORMATION
In 1517 a German theologian Martin Luther nailed a list of 97 protests against abuses in the Church. Printing spread his ideas and Protestant churches sprang up in all parts of Europe, taking particular root in Germany, England and Scandinavia. The key slogan was 'Sola Fide', (Latin for 'By Faith Alone'), i.e. not by doing good deeds. The Bible became available in the language of the people. The Roman Catholic Church met in the Council of Trent (1545-1563) to purify itself from abuses. Both Protestants and Catholics hardened their theology and religious wars broke out which lasted for more than a hundred years.

MISSIONS
In the 16th century the Catholic Church sent Jesuit missionaries to the Far East and South America. In the 19th century Protestant missionaries followed, especially to Africa. In the 20th century new

Pentecostal churches were created throughout the world so that now over 50% of Christians live in the global South. Christians in 2022 total 2.56 billion or 31% of the world's population.

BIBLE, TRADITION, REASON

Christians are not only divided between different churches, but divided within them, from those who interpret their faith through reason, often called liberals, to those who maintain that the Bible should be read and believed literally, often called evangelicals. The former see faith as a way of making sense of life, acknowledging the insights of science and historical scholarship, the latter see it as a personal relationship with Jesus. Both aim to keep the faith.

EASTERN CHRISTIANITY

WHERE
The heartland of Eastern Christianity is what used to be the Eastern Roman Empire: Greece and the Middle East, plus Bulgaria, Romania, Ukraine and Russia. Since 1900 an Eastern diaspora has spread worldwide. Eastern Christianity follows an unbroken tradition originating in the undivided church of the fourth century.

SCHISMS
The Council of Chalcedon, 451, created a major schism. Rome and Constantinople agreed that Christ had two natures, God and man, while Antioch and Alexandria affirmed only one combined nature. These churches have been separated ever since.

The barbarian invasions of the 4th and 5th centuries and the Muslim conquests of the 7th split the western church speaking Latin from the eastern church speaking Greek. Differences in theology and politics finally created schism in the late 11th century. The dreadful capture of Constantinople by the crusaders in 1204 made reconciliation virtually impossible.

MISSION
The great age of missionary activity by the Orthodox Church was in the ninth century. Two brothers, Cyril and Methodius, (d.869 and 885) translated the Bible and service books into Slavonic, thus helping grow Orthodox churches in Serbia, Romania, Bulgaria and Russia.

PERSECUTION
From the rise of Islam in the 7th century, and especially after the Turkish capture of Constantinople in1453, most Orthodox Christians have been second-class citizens or 'dhimmis', suffering occasional outbursts of violence. Over a million Armenian and Syriac Christians were killed by the Ottomans in 1915-17 and two million Greek Christians expelled in 1922.

The Communist Revolution in Russia created aggressively atheist states in Eastern Europe up to 1989 in which hundreds of churches were closed and priests imprisoned.

WORSHIP
In 987 the Prince of Rus sent envoys to research different religions. In Constantinople they witnessed the Divine Liturgy and *"knew not whether we were in heaven or on earth, for surely there is no such splendour or beauty anywhere upon earth… This we know, that God dwells there among humans."* Orthodox worship is still famous for its music, chanted unaccompanied, and decorative splendour. Everyone stands, allowing freedom to move and kiss an icon or even leave for a while.

ICONS

The iconoclastic controversy, 726 to 843, arose between those wanting to eradicate idolatry and those affirming that God works through the material world. In the end statues were discouraged, but icons, 2D images of saints 'written' in prayer, were declared proper channels of grace. An Orthodox church today is filled with icons. *"God can be depicted because He became human and took on flesh"* (Ware - The Orthodox Church p.33).

HOLY SPIRIT

"The true aim of the Christian life is the acquisition of the Holy Spirit of God." (Seraphim of Sarov, 1754-1833).

Between 579 and 1014 the Western Church added 'Filioque' ('and the Son') to the Nicene Creed's statement that the Holy Spirit proceeds from the Father. The Orthodox Churches never accepted it because it was not agreed by a council of the whole church. The original statement safeguards the belief that *"God enters into a direct and immediate relationship with humankind… Deification is…the normal goal for every Christian without exception"* (Ware pp. 68, 229).

ISLAM

THE BEGINNING
Muhammad (peace be upon him) received the first revelation from God in 610 CE. Muslims were persecuted by the people of Makkah (Mecca), so they emigrated to Medina in 622 CE, year 0 of the Muslim calendar. Muhammad (pbuh) received the submission of Makkah in 630 CE, two years before he died.

BELIEFS
Allah
Central to islam is the oneness (tawhid) of God or Allah. He is transcendent, beyond comprehension. Anything which confuses the oneness of Allah is idolatry.

The prophets
Islam recognises all the prophets recorded in the Bible, from Adam, through Abraham/Ibrahim to Isa/Jesus. However, Muhammad (pbuh) is called 'the Seal of the Prophets' and no further revelation is needed.

The books
Allah (God) gave revelations through the Torah and

the Gospel but they have become distorted. The Qur'an ('recitation') was revealed to Mohammed (pbuh) by the archangel Jibril/Gabriel in words directly imparted by the Divine. Consequently it only exists in the original Arabic. All translations are interpretations. Accounts of Muhammad's (pbuh) life and teaching were recorded in the hadith. These help with interpreting the Qur'an.

Angels
Angels are a multitude of created heavenly beings, different angels having different tasks.

The Day of Resurrection
At an unknown date there will be a day of judgement in which *'whoever does an atom's weight of good will see it. And whoever does an atom's weight of evil will see it'* (Surah al-Zalzalah). All humankind will be consigned to paradise or hell.

Fate
Every matter, good or bad, has been decreed by God.

THE FIVE PILLARS
Shahada/declaration of faith
"I testify that there is no god but Allah/God and I testify that Muhammad is the messenger of Allah." To convert to Islam one has merely to say the Shahada.

Salah/Prayer
Muslims are normally required to pray five times a day, reciting prayers and the Qur'an accompanied by bowing and prostrating oneself.

Zakat/Alms Giving
For those who can afford it, 2.5% of annual wealth is to be given to the poor and needy.

Fasting
During the month of Ramadan Muslims are required to have nothing to eat or drink from sunrise to sunset. Because Islam uses a lunar calendar, Ramadan comes earlier annually by about ten days.

Hajj/Pilgrimage
All Muslims who can afford it are required to make the annual pilgrimage to Mecca once in their lives, recreating the Islamic story of Ibrahim/Abraham.

DIVISIONS OF ISLAM
Sunni
Sunni Islam comprises 85% of the Muslim world. It accepts the first three caliphs, Abu Bakr, Umar and Uthman. It includes both traditional Islam and more extreme and fundamentalist movements such as Salahism and Wahhabism as in Saudi Arabia.

Shia
Shia Islam dates from a battle in 657 CE when the prophet's son-in-law Ali was killed. Shia allocates spiritual authority to the family of Muhammad (pbuh). 10-15% of Muslims adhere to it, mainly in Iran, Iraq and Lebanon.

Sufism
Sufism is Islam's mystical-ascetic tradition, aimed at the purification of the inner self.

SIKHI
ALSO KNOWN AS SIKHISM

THE TEN GURUS
Guru Nanak (1469-1539 CE) was born in the Punjab in modern-day Pakistan. The religion of the people was Hindu, though the ruling class was Muslim. and had been for three hundred years. From childhood Nanak had a deep devotion to God, and after a spiritual revelation spent twenty years walking throughout India proclaiming, *"There is no Hindu, no Musalmaan".* He then worked as a farmer and established the first centre of Sikhism. (Sikh means disciple or student). Throughout his life he sang of the sacred splendour of the Almighty through his hymns. At the end of his life he handed his spiritual authority to Guru Angad. The line of succession continued to the tenth guru, Gobind Singh (1666-1708) who declared that the eleventh guru would be the collected prayers and hymns of Guru Nanak and his successors, called Sri Guru Granth Sahib.

SRI GURU GRANTH SAHIB
The Guru Granth Sahib is the Sikhs' eternal Guru, literally meaning the Holy Book of the Spiritual

Enlightener and Master. It is a collection of hymns of the first five Gurus, the Ninth Guru, and various saints totalling 1430 pages (or 'limbs') and 5,894 hymns. It is source of all Sikh prayer. It enshrines the core beliefs of Sikhism including faith and meditation in the name of the one creator, the equality of all humankind; the duty of seva ('selfless service') while living a householder's life. In Sikh gurdwaras, or temples, it is treated as a living person and is venerated by the devotees.

NITNEM

Nitnem means daily routine, reciting the daily prayers. These are taken entirely from the Guru Granth Sahib. They include the long Japji Sahib composed by Guru Nanak, and the Benti Chaupai, a short bani of 54 lines composed by Guru Gobind Singh. Devout Sikhs will recite the five 'banis' between 3.00 and 6.00 in the morning; this takes about 25 minutes.There are also prayers in the evening and before bed. Ideally prayer should be continuous.

KHALSA

Sikhs suffered persecution from the Mughal emperors. Two of the ten gurus were tortured and executed as were tenth guru Gobind Singh's two sons. In 1699 Gobind Singh instituted a new fraternity of saint-soldiers called Khalsa who underwent Baptism - Amrit Initiation, and took the surname Singh (lion) or Kaur (princess). Khalsa means 'pure and sovereign'. Apart from wearing the turban, Khalsa Sikhs wear the 'five Ks':

- kes (uncut hair)
- kangha (small wooden comb)
- kachh (cotton breeches)

- kirpan (sword/dagger)
- kara (iron bangle)

The inauguration of the Khalsa is celebrated each year in mid- April.

SEVA

Seva means selfless service. For Sikhs God is within all of us, and by serving humanity one is serving God's creation; also seva helps control inner vices and brings us closer to God. Sikhism stresses honest work and sharing, most visibly in providing communal food kitchens where volunteers prepare and serve vegetarian meals to all.

As Guru Nanak taught, *"Truth is the highest virtue, but higher still is truthful living."*

ALCOHOLICS ANONYMOUS

WHY?
Why is Alcoholics Anonymous included in this book of prayers from the world's major faiths? It is emphatically not a religion. It has no creed, no formal membership, and only the loosest of organisational structures. However, it is a spiritual path, one that can be embraced by agnostics and by people of faith without distinction.

Richard Rohr, an American Franciscan said, *"I believe that Jesus and the Twelve Steps of Alcoholics Anonymous are saying the same thing but with different vocabulary: We suffer to get well. We surrender to win. We die to live. We give it away to keep it."*

THE BEGINNING
In June 1935 an alcoholic stockbroker Bill W, six months sober, talked to an alcoholic doctor, Bob S, about a spiritual solution to their common problem. The principles came from a radical Christian organisation, the Oxford Groups, later Moral Re-armament. The key, unique element was that the message was carried

from one alcoholic to another. Groups formed in Akron and New York. With over a hundred alcoholics finding sobriety, they published a book in 1939 describing the programme and experiences entitled 'Alcoholics Anonymous'. This became the name the society.

THE PROGRAMME

Bill W summed up the programme in four words: 'Trust God. Clean House.'

The book lays out the twelve steps of the programme. The first three are crucial:

1. We admitted we were powerless over alcohol – that our lives had become unmanageable.

2. Came to believe that a Power greater than ourselves could restore us to sanity.

3. Made a decision to turn our will and our lives over to the care of God as we understood Him.

Other steps include:

- making a 'searching and fearless' moral inventory;
- sharing our inventory with God and with another human being;
- making direct amends to all we had harmed;
- improving our conscious contact with God through prayer and meditation;
- carrying the message to others.

GOD?

When Bill's friend Ebby T had passed the message on, Bill was hostile to any mention of God. Ebby said "Why don't you choose your own conception of God?"

Bill got it. 'It was only a matter of being willing to believe in a Power greater than myself. Nothing more was required of me to make my beginning.'

The chapter on 'We Agnostics' says, *'If (you are probably alcoholic), you may be suffering from an illness that only a spiritual experience will conquer... Our own conception, however inadequate, was sufficient to make the approach and to effect a contact with Him... To us, the Realm of Spirit is broad, roomy, all inclusive... It is open, we believe, to all.'*

THE SPREAD

AA has groups in 180 countries with an estimated membership of two million.

There are separate 12 step groups for those suffering from substance addictions such as Nicotine, Narcotics, Cocaine, Heroin, Marijuana and Crystal meth.

There are several groups for sufferers of process addictions, addictions of the mind, such as Co-Dependents, Gamblers, Overeaters, Sex Addicts, Sex and Love Addicts and Workaholics.

There are also twelve steps groups for those suffering the effects of someone else's addiction, such as Al-Anon (started by Bill W's wife Lois), COSA (Co-dependents of Sex Addicts) and Gam-Anon.

As the preface to the first edition of Alcoholics stated: *'We are sure that our way of life has its advantages for all.'*

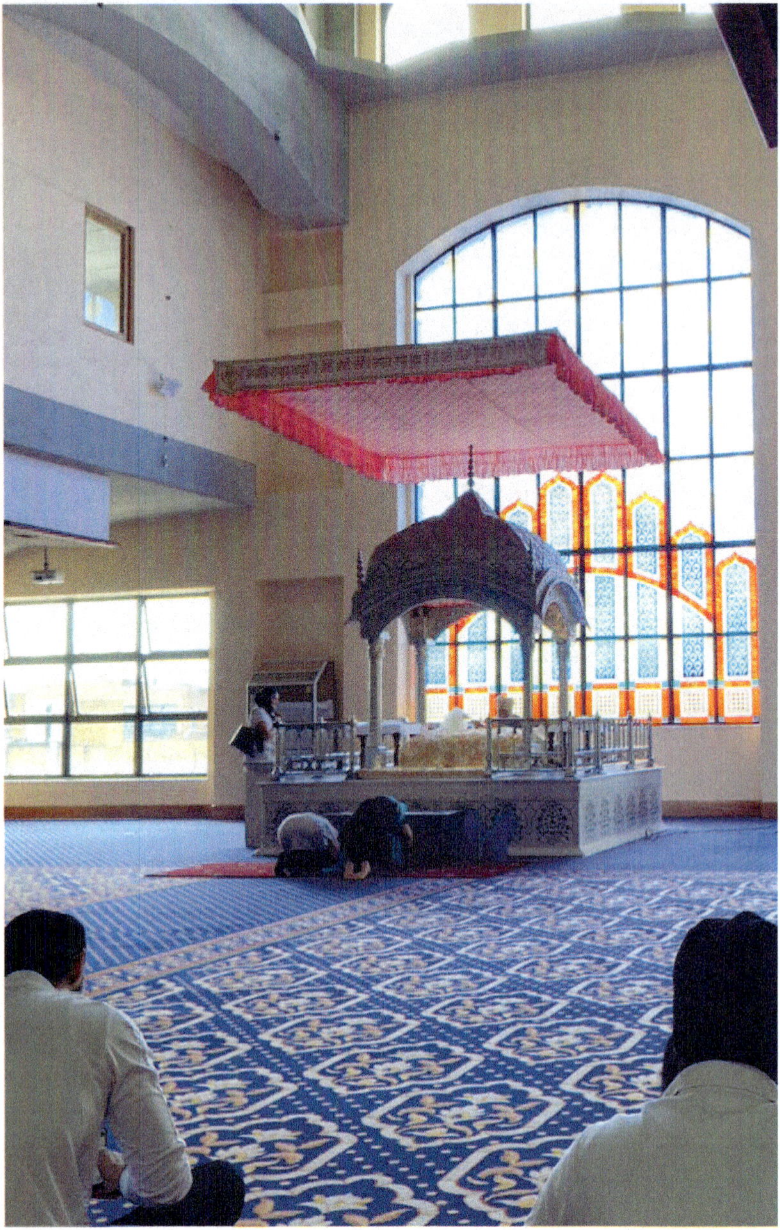

SIKH PRAYER

I explained earlier that for Sikhs prayer is the recitation of the five 'banis' or hymns in the morning, with more in the evening. Recitation of the five banis, or listening to them on headphones takes about twenty five minutes.

Below is the beginning of the fundamental prayer of Sikhism, the Japji Singh composed by Guru Nanak in the 15th century. This is about one eighth of the whole prayer.

JAP JI SAHIB

One Universal Creator God. The Name Is Truth.
Creative Being Personified. No Fear. No Hatred.
Image Of The Undying, Beyond Birth, Self-Existent.
By Guru's Grace ~

True In The Primal Beginning. True Throughout The Ages.
True Here And Now. O Nanak, Forever And Ever True.
By thinking, He cannot be reduced to thought, even by thinking hundreds of thousands of times.

*By remaining silent, inner silence is not obtained, even by remaining lovingly absorbed deep within
The hunger of the hungry is not appeased, even by piling up loads of worldly goods.
Hundreds of thousands of clever tricks, but not even one of them will go along with you in the end.
So how can you become truthful? And how can the veil of illusion be torn away?
O Nanak, it is written that you shall obey the Hukam of His Command, and walk in the Way of His Will.
By His Command, bodies are created; His Command cannot be described.
By His Command, souls come into being; by His Command, glory and greatness are obtained.
By His Command, some are high and some are low; by His Written Command, pain and pleasure are obtained.
Some, by His Command, are blessed and forgiven; others, by His Command, wander aimlessly forever.
Everyone is subject to His Command; no one is beyond His Command.*

*O Nanak, one who understands His Command, does not speak in ego.
Some sing of His Power - who has that Power?
Some sing of His Gifts, and know His Sign and Insignia.
Some sing of His Glorious Virtues, Greatness and Beauty.*

*Some sing of knowledge obtained of Him, through difficult philosophical studies.
Some sing that He fashions the body, and then again reduces it to dust.
Some sing that He takes life away, and then again restores it.*

Some sing that He seems so very far away.
Some sing that He watches over us, face to face,
ever-present.

There is no shortage of those who preach and teach.
Millions upon millions offer millions of sermons and
stories.
The Great Giver keeps on giving, while those who
receive grow weary of receiving.
Throughout the ages, consumers consume.
The Commander, by His Command, leads us to walk
on the Path.

O Nanak, He blossoms forth, Carefree and Untroubled.
True is the Master, True is His Name-speak it with
infinite love.
People beg and pray, "Give to us, give to us",
and the Great Giver gives His Gifts.
So what offering can we place before Him,
by which we might see the Darbaar of His Court?
What words can we speak to evoke His Love?
In the Amrit Vaylaa, the ambrosial hours before
dawn, chant the True Name, and contemplate His
Glorious Greatness.

By the karma of past actions, the robe of this
physical body is obtained. By His Grace, the Gate of
Liberation is found.

O Nanak, know this well: the True One Himself is All.
He cannot be established, He cannot be created.
He Himself is Immaculate and Pure.
Those who serve Him are honoured.

O Nanak, sing of the Lord, the Treasure of
Excellence...

PHOTOS

'Praying Hands', Albrecht Dürer (1471-1528)	1
Mount Everest	2
Andy Roland	4
Fountains Abbey, North Yorkshire	14
Monastery of the Holy Trinity, Crawley Down	20
Teaspoon	24
Day of the Dead, Kew Gardens	28
View from Bolton Castle, North Yorkshire	32
Nidaros Cathedral, Trondheim, Norway	36
Pegnitz River, Nuremberg, Bavaria	40
Sky	44
Crib at San Salvatore, Jerusalem	48
Gurdwara Sri Guru Singh Sabha, Southall	90

All photos by the author, except Praying Hands and Mount Everest (free-to-use).

OTHER BOOKS BY REV ANDY ROLAND

The following books can all be purchased through **bibleinbrief.org, revandybooks.org** or Amazon

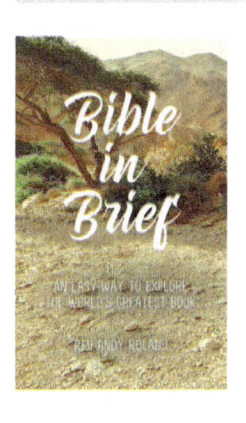

BIBLE IN BRIEF

"This book does what few others do – it offers a very helpful guide for those looking for a brief overview of the Bible and its story."
Bishop Graham Tomlin

Bible in Brief gives a comprehensive overview of the Bible in six months with each month covering a separate topic:

- Genesis and Exodus
- History of Israel and Judah
- Prophets
- Law, Psalms and Wisdom
- Jesus
- Apostles and their Letters

There are daily readings with a question each day to help us engage with it. There are also maps, timelines and an archaeological drawing for each week.

At the end of each month there is a section called 'The Other Side', with quotations from the surrounding cultures.

The book can be also be used alongside the website on one's phone.

"There has never been a sustained and powerful renewal of Christian faith without a renewed engagement with the Bible. Andy Roland provides a practical introduction to a lifetime relationship with the word of God."
Rt Revd Richard Chartres, former Bishop of London

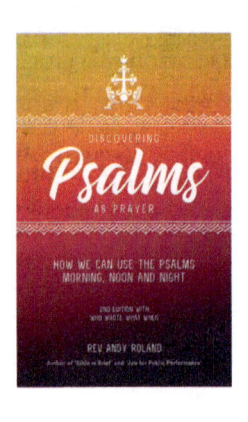

DISCOVERING PSALMS AS PRAYER

Forty years ago Andy Roland spent a couple of days in a Christian ashram in south India. Attending just one morning service revolutionised his approach to the psalms and how he could actually pray them.

'Discovering Psalms as Prayer describes how psalms can enrich our prayers when we get up, at lunchtime, in the evening and at night.

"In 'Discovering Psalms as Prayer' Andy Roland weaves together the wisdom of a faithful, personal pilgrimage with practical guidance for reading the Psalms. It will be a gift to those wanting to make that discovery for themselves. We are in his debt."
Rev David Runcorn, author of 'Spirituality Workbook - a Guide for Explorers, Pilgrims and Seekers'

Also available on audio.

JESUS THE TROUBLEMAKER

Jesus the Troublemaker is a historical novel of the last days of Jesus' life.

Jesus is placed firmly in his Jewish context as a Galilean rabbi. He is called by his actual, Aramaic name, Yeshua, as are all the others in the story.

By closely following the evidence, Andy Roland sheds a whole new light on what Jesus/Yeshua actually did in his last week on earth. Lively dialogues help us hear his words afresh

Maps and illustrations provided an aid in imagining the events.

"Well! Holy Week has come alive in a new way and will never be the same again. The book has finally removed set images and confusions stuck in my mind from so many years and something much more vibrant and alive has replaced them. I especially appreciated the trial scenes and the final hours of Jesus life."
Sr Hilda Mary CSC, St Michael's Convent

"I much enjoyed reading Jesus the Troublemaker during Holy Week."
Dr Michael Ipgrave, Bishop of Lichfield

"An interesting and challenging book."
Rabbi Helen Freeman, West London Synagogue

Also available on audio.

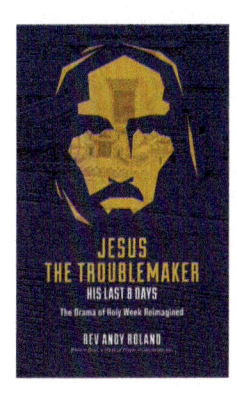

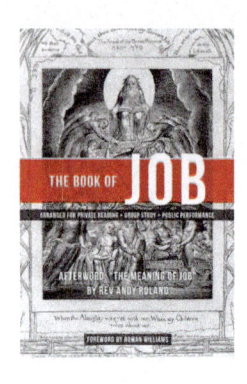

THE BOOK OF JOB, WITH ESSAY 'THE MEANING OF JOB'

This work consists of

a) a week of personal readings;

b) a group study in which the whole of the book can be experienced in a single session; and

c) a version for public performance, 75 minutes with musical interludes.

The book is illustrated with William Blake's etchings.

"To understand anything about how the book works, we need to hear it as drama, as an exchange of passionate, difficult speeches. Hence the importance of this 'arrangement', which allows us to enter the space of the writer's imagination and the writer's faith as it is tested, pushed and squeezed, almost rejected, revived, articulated in intense protest and equally intense trust."
from the foreword by Rowan Williams

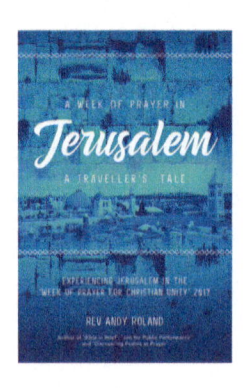

A WEEK OF PRAYER IN JERUSALEM

A travel diary of Rev Andy's participation in the Week of Prayer for Christian Unity in Jerusalem in 2017 - his seventh visit. He describes all eight of the unity services held in a wide variety churches from Lutheran to Ethiopian Orthodox. He also visits the holy sites, the Israel Museum, Tel Aviv and Bethlehem. There are entertaining anecdotes of his meetings with Jerusalem residents over the years. Fully illustrated with colour photos taken by the author.

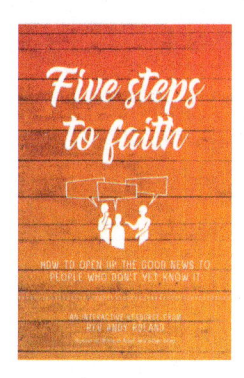

FIVE STEPS TO FAITH
A tested pastoral programme introducing families to the Christian story in their own homes in just five weeks.

Each session includes a film, two Bible passages, explained simply by asking the right questions and ending with a fitting prayer.

Perfect to offer families who are thinking of having their child baptised/christened. It works!

Suggested resources are downloadable from **bibleinbrief.org**

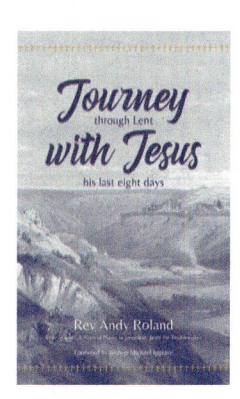

JOURNEY THROUGH LENT WITH JESUS
For fifty days we accompany Jesus from the Jordan valley, up to Jerusalem and eventually to the cross and beyond. Each day has a Bible passage; part of the historical novel 'Jesus the Troublemaker' setting the scene; a Biblical comment; a personal reflection and a suggestion of something to do. Fully illustrated.

"The joy of this book is that, even as it establishes the strangeness of the Messianic story, it also provides lots of ways through which its unsettling and transforming power can reach deep inside us: reimagined dialogue, personal anecdote, historical explanation, spiritual guidance are all there to hook the story and its reality into our lives."
Dr Michael Ipgrave, Bishop of Lichfield